MW00941439

Before You Are Licensed

13 Actions to Jump Start
Your Future Real Estate Career

Katherine Scarim

Disclaimer:

First and foremost, it is *illegal* to practice real estate without a license. You should never engage in any activity that would mislead the public into believing you are a licensed real estate agent. The suggestions in this book are intended to allow you to start gaining knowledge and mapping out your future real estate business—**not** to have you begin your career prior to licensure.

The reader is solely responsible for adhering to all international, federal, state, and local professional licensing laws and other business regulations. The author/publisher specifically disclaim any liability, loss, or risk which is incurred as a consequence directly or indirectly, of the use and application of any of the contents of this work.

So, while the suggestions should increase the likelihood of quicker success, I make no guarantees as to your earning potential based on the content of this book. Your financial success solely depends on you – but then again, that's kind of exciting, isn't it?

Contents

Hit the Ground Running

The real estate industry has an unnecessarily high washout rate. It is common to see agents leave the business before their first anniversary. Make it five years in real estate, and you are considered an old timer.

Why the high turnover? More often than not, it can be attributed to new agents running out of money before they have had time to build a successful business.

Brokers and veteran agents alike will preach the ever-sage advice that new agents should put away three to six months of savings. It will hold them over until their first sale and allow their business to gain momentum. Sound advice.

However, I have yet to meet anyone who intentionally and successfully stored away the recommended funds prior to starting in real estate.

I call bull.

Those same brokers and agents espousing such wisdom most likely did not follow it themselves. Perhaps they had a spouse with a steady income that allowed for some breathing room. Maybe they continued a "day job" until their real estate business picked up. I'm willing to guess some were on the brink of quitting when that first transaction miraculously closed, giving them a bit more time.

So I am going to give you actual advice that can provide you with early success in real estate. If you succeed quickly, you won't have to quit. It's that simple.

If you plan to succeed, you need to hit the ground running. This seems obvious, but in our industry the average agent will spend the bulk of the first six "make it or break it" months on non-income-producing activities.

So let's stop the madness.

"I'm going to get my real estate license after the kids finish preschool."

"I retire in six months. Then I'm going to get my real estate license."

"I can't stand my job. After we get our annual bonuses, I'm going to quit and get my real estate license."

That's all good and fine, but in the meantime, there is nothing stopping you from acquiring market knowledge, researching brokerages, nurturing a future client base, creating marketing materials for future use, increasing your social media presence. . . the list goes on and on.

So it's your choice:

Wait until you are licensed and living on borrowed time to begin to lay the foundation for your future business and run the high risk becoming a statistic.

Or you can read on and secure your future.

Learn Your Market

In the real estate industry, the strongest agents are always conducting "inventory." They consistently visit new homes listed for sale, regardless of whether they have a current client looking for that type of home. Why? So that when engaged in conversations, they will have quick, house-specific responses: "I was just in 123 Main Street. It's exactly what you are looking for. Would you like me to set up a showing for us?" Who wouldn't want to work with that agent?

1.)   Visit model homes

Builders go to great lengths and expense to determine what today's buyers want. Remember, the closer you can stage a resale home to resemble model homes in your area, the higher the price it is likely to fetch.

How would you describe the floor plan (open concept, traditional, etc.)?

Kitchens and bathrooms sell a home. Note the type and style of appliances. Observe the height, quantity, finish, and style of the cabinets. Determine the ratio of bathrooms to bedrooms.

What colors, finishes, and materials are used throughout the home?

Is the décor traditional or modern? Are the furniture sizes standard or oversized?

If situated in a planned division with a representative on-site, explain that you are working on getting your real estate license and simply learning the area inventory. Do not mislead the representative into believing you are a prospective buyer or licensed agent.

Ask the following questions:

When is the last home expected to be completed?

How many lots are currently available?

Which lots are more desirable and higher in cost?

Are additional phases planned?

What is the typical build time?

Is, or will, the community be gated or have a security patrol?

Is there a mandatory homeowners' association fee? Is it paid monthly, quarterly, annually? What does it pay for?

Is there an available list of rules and regulations homeowners will be required to follow?

Are you allowed to take pictures of the subdivision marque, amenities, or exterior spaces for future use in your marketing?

Collect all the available brochures, floor plans, and flyers.

Prior to leaving, visit the clubhouse and any amenities offered.

Walk or drive the streets. Are any streets cul-de-sacs? Are there sidewalks? How closely are the homes situated? Are they positioned on the front or rear of the lots? Are mailboxes individual to the homes or in groupings?

Once home, create a file for the subdivision or builder. Fill it with any printed materials you were given and any notes you may have taken. Study the pricing differences and memorize the model names and floor plans. Research the builder's online reviews and check the Better Business Bureau for complaints. If you were allowed to take photos, save them on your computer under a matching subdivision or builder file.

2.)   Visit open houses

Open houses, especially for a new agent in need of clients, provide an excellent way to meet buyers (and occasionally sellers). Visit as many open houses as you can. During my first year of real estate, with the exception of one client, I worked with buyers that I met at open houses.

One day soon, you will be holding open houses. Applying what you saw that worked and avoiding what turned you off will help you hold better open houses and impress prospective clients faster.

*   **Study how open houses are found in your area.**

    Do they appear in the papers?

    Are they solely online?

    Have you ever been mailed an invitation to one? I love this strategy for getting neighbors to attend. It works twofold: Shy neighbors are more likely to attend if they were "personally invited," and neighbors who are considering selling their own homes will favorably remember your unique marketing and commitment to getting people through the door.

    How early are directional signs put out in the neighborhoods?

    Which directional signs catch your eye? Why?

    How is the actual home marked? Balloons? Banner?

- **Observe active real estate agents working open houses.**

Are you greeted when you enter? How?

Is there a sign-in sheet or iPad setup available for you to leave your contact information? What information does it ask for? Did the agent prompt you to sign in? If so, how?

If there are potential buyers viewing the home when you arrive, do not interrupt the agent. As you walk the home, try to stay within earshot but out of the way (perhaps in the next room) and listen to how he or she interacts with the prospective buyers.

Do the visitors seem engaged? Impressed?

Does the agent seem calm, knowledgeable, uncertain, bored, or frantic? Why?

Is the agent quick with answers or unprepared to field them?

Are the agent's interactions more emotional/superficial in nature? For example, "Don't you just *LOVE* the staircase?" Or do they focus more on value added? For example, "Residents also get to enjoy eight lighted tennis courts and a heated Olympic-size pool."

What did the agent do or say that impressed you?

What would you have done or said differently if you were the agent?

Of great import: if you needed a real estate agent, would you be inclined to use this agent?

Do you receive any follow up correspondence from the agent as a result of having signed in? How many days later were you contacted? Was it via phone, email, or postal mail? Did it make you want to re-engage with the agent?

- **Interact with active real estate agents at their open houses.**

If you are lucky enough to happen upon an agent sitting in an empty open house, strike up a conversation! Explain that you are thinking about entering real estate and want to learn about the market. Get the agent talking. Great questions to ask:

How long have you been in the business?

Do you love it? Why or why not?

How many hours do you typically work per week?

Which brokerage firm do you hang your license with?

Do you like your co-workers?

Why did you choose that firm?

Do you have a close relationship with your broker?

Did you ever work at any other firms? Why did you leave?

Do you work more with buyers or sellers?
What is the one thing you wish you had been told before you entered real estate?

Let the conversation flow organically.

If the agent is quick to shut it down because you are not a prospective buyer, thank him or her, walk the home, and be on your way. But it might be wise to note the firm the agent works for. Is that the type of person you'd like as your co-worker?

If the conversation goes great, the agent will tell you to call if you have any additional questions or invite you to coffee. Take up the offer (and thank the agent by accommodating his or her schedule and buying the coffee). True real estate professionals find joy in helping others and value relationships.

- **Study the home**

Experience and study the open houses in much the same way you did the model homes. However, with resale homes you are also going to have to note condition, age, and curb appeal, as these are major factors in resale pricing.

Thinking back to model homes you have visited, could the resale home have been staged better? How?

3.)   Visit For Sale By Owner (FSBO) open houses

Experience and study the FSBO open houses in much the same way you did the agent open houses. However, pay attention to how differently owners interact with prospective buyers.

Often owners are more emotional in their interactions. They are quick to take offense and often highlight features of the property that are personal to them but not important to the buyer. Moreover, staging attempts often fall short or are non-existent.

One day you will have to explain to FSBOs why a professional real estate agent will likely get a better price for their home than their own efforts. You will have many examples to draw on from your FSBO open house inventory experiences.

4.) Read and analyze online and print local home sale advertisements

What was it about the photo(s) that appealed to you? Did anything about the photos turn you off?

Did the text answer all your questions about the property, or did it leave you wanting to learn more?

Did you care for the choice of descriptive words?

Pay attention to the prices. Over time, you will get a general feel for the asking prices in different areas and for the prices of certain types of homes.

Does the agent's photo appear in the ad? Do you like the photo?

Does the agent include a tagline in the ad? For example, "Your waterfront specialist." Does the tagline add or detract from the ad?

Create a file of "better ads" to refer to in the future.

5.) Familiarize yourself with local town and county municipal web sites

Sites that provide property-specific documents are often available through the county clerk, tax appraiser's office, building departments, and zoning and/or planning departments.

Save the links to your bookmarks or desktop for future ease of reference. You will visit them often once you are working transactions.

Learn what documents are available for public review and if there are any procedures you must go through to obtain them. For example, some entities may require that you accept an online disclaimer, submit a Freedom of Information Act (FOIA) request, and/or pay copying fees before they are released.

6.)   Study local architecture and desirable features in your area

You will need to be able to differentiate between local home styles and intelligently discuss the pros and cons of each layout. Architecture and home plan books can be excellent resources.

Each home style has a history behind it and usually a few fun facts as well. Memorize a few facts to sprinkle into a client conversation every now and then. For example, mansard roofs are named after the French renaissance architect Mansart. Portions of the Louvre have mansard roofs.

If your area includes a large amount of new construction, you must also have a working knowledge of the different builders and their reputations. Some builder information can be obtained during your model home visits.

Moreover, you are going to have to identify which features of each home are more or less desirable to the local buyer, allowing for proper seller pricing and buyer negotiations.

Learn what the features typically cost in material, installation, and/or upkeep, and research variations or options of the features. Do this by visiting showrooms and home improvement stores, calling contractors, and asking friends or neighbors who have these features in their homes.

For example, in Florida, private pools are extremely desirable features. Florida agents are expected to be knowledgeable about swimming pools. You'd better be quick on your toes to answer buyer questions about whether the yard is large enough to accommodate a pool; the average cost of a small vs. large pool; the additional cost for hot tub; solar vs. gas heat; the typical ratio of pool to patio; etc.

7.) Learn at least one town inside and out

While you might think you know your town intimately, it is more likely that you only know what your town has to offer someone your age, within your circle of friends, and with your interests.

Start with a good old-fashioned map. Really study it. Highlight the streets and parks that you have never travelled. And then hit the road! Travel the streets over the course of a couple of days, or just make a point every time you are driving somewhere to take a new route.

When you drive residential streets, ask yourself:

What is the traffic like?

Do the yards look well kept?

Do any of the homes have views (golf course, lake, ocean, forest preserve)?

Do the homes appear uniform in style?

Do the homes appear uniform in age?

Do the homes appear equally kept up?

Is there a mix of single- and multi-family homes?

Is there a mix of residential and commercial properties?

Every now and then, stop and take a photo with a long street view to file with your other future marketing photos. Do not take photos while standing on private property—only when on public land or right-of-ways.

When you visit parks, memorize what they have to offer (playgrounds, restrooms, kayak rentals, etc.). Be certain to photograph the park, especially pretty areas and unique features.

Try different restaurants. Out-of-town buyers will, at some point, ask their agent to recommend a restaurant. Know the different types of ethnic restaurants in the area. Be ready to name a couple of special occasion (fine dining) restaurants. Kid-friendly restaurants and good breakfast spots are also asked about often. Order an interesting dish and take a photo. Also, photograph the fronts of the more interesting restaurants. Some of the photos might work great on the community page of your future real estate website.

As stated before, up until now, you have only used your town according to your needs and desires. Step outside of yourself and brainstorm ideas about what buyers with different needs and interests would want to know, and thus likely ask you about, when moving to your town. Then seek out the answers. For example (the possibilities are endless):

- Dog owners – locations and hours of dog parks, pet stores, leash laws, recommendations for a veterinarian, knowledge of which homeowner or condo associations allow dogs.

- Families with children – schools, playgrounds, tutoring centers, babysitter recommendations, pediatrician recommendations, sports programs, music programs.

- Boaters – number and/or locations of fixed bridges, locations and hours of public boat launches, cost and availability of boat storage, bait shop locations and hours.

Last, attend local town meetings. There is no better way to learn who runs your town, what developments are being planned, what concerns are being addressed, and about the current strength of the economy. Most meetings are open to the public.

Assuming you follow the advice above, imagine how much sooner after licensing you will be able to honestly call yourself a "local real estate expert" as opposed to the other new agents (and sadly, some that have been practicing for years).

New Construction Communities to Visit:

_____
_____
_____
_____
_____
_____
_____
_____
_____
_____

Local Architectural Styles to Study:

_____
_____
_____
_____
_____
_____
_____
_____
_____

Local Attractions and Restaurants to Experience:

_____
_____
_____
_____
_____
_____
_____
_____
_____

Nurture and Increase Your Future Client Base

You must learn to be selective as to who you will work with. Clients are different from headaches.

Headaches don't respect your time, and they view you as replaceable. You will know a headache when you meet one. They refuse to get pre-qualified, try to pit you against other agents, and don't respond to your communications – yet expect you to jump when they want to see a home. You do not want headaches.

Clients, on the other hand, value your time and knowledge. They are grateful that you are honest and professional. Better yet, clients recommend you to other clients.

8.)   Organize your spheres

In real estate, you will constantly hear talk about "Your Spheres of Influence." Simply put, you have circles of acquaintances based on different aspects of your life.

While some agents lump their contacts, regardless of what sphere they originated from, into buyers or sellers categories (i.e. six months from purchase or two years out for selling), I believe that future agents should have their contacts organized by sphere.

Most new agents wrongly assume that their friends and family will use them for their real estate needs. The truth is, buying or selling a home is stressful because, well, a home is typically the largest investment a person has. It is also true that your friends and family know all too well that you are brand new and know nothing about real estate transactions. So while they might want to support your career ambitions, they don't necessarily want to jeopardize their home sale or purchase.

I don't think there is an agent out there that hasn't been blindsided when their sister, friend, neighbor, even parent, used another agent. Try not to let it upset you or affect your relationship with the person.

If you are going to be successful in real estate, you will have to learn how to shake off rejection and look for the next opportunity. Forgive them in your heart and move on. Just wait. They'll use you when you have a couple of years behind you and they are ready to buy or sell again.

So we need to speed up how long it takes your existing spheres to trust you.

Nurture and Increase Your Future Client Base

The fastest way to overcome your friends' and family's concerns about your being new to real estate is to organize your contacts by sphere.

That way, when you get licensed, you can market to them in a way that reminds them of your personality traits or the existing skills that you bring with you to your new career.

The average new agent will, on their brokerage's suggestion, send out a general, "I got my real estate license, and I hope you'll use me . . . " letter to every person they know. In my opinion, this screams, "Hey, I'm new. I'm testing our friendship/relationship to see if you'll use me. Let me know."

Yikes.

Instead, group your future clients into spheres and write individual letters for each group.

Groups may include, for example, former work colleagues, neighbors, congregation members, and college friends.

Once the groups have been sorted, draft letters accordingly.

Should you be lucky enough to be leaving another real estate-related industry, make the connection clear for the reader.

- "Having spent the last ten years working in construction, I am well aware of what to look for to determine if a home is structurally sound."

- "Having spent three years selling mortgages, I am well versed in what possible glitches can occur during the home purchase process and am well equipped to get them resolved."

If you are unable to make a connection directly to the real estate industry, remind them of your complementary personality traits.

- "I plan to utilize my strong organizational skills and my attention to details to protect my clients through clean contract work. I'm sure you remember my merciless accounting during the spring fun fair. I apologize if, as a volunteer, it drove you nuts, but it will be of great benefit to my clients!"

- "Hopefully, when you think of me and our years working together at ACME Company, my intense dedication to customer satisfaction and my strong communication skills come to mind. I have every intention of utilizing them for each and every one of my future real estate clients' benefit."

Save your letters. The minute you are licensed and have joined a brokerage, copy and paste your letters onto the brokerage letterhead to mail or email.

Over time, you will begin sending group-specific updates about your successes. Of greatest value is when you get your first recommendation from within the group – that's just pure gold.

9.) Research local social clubs, networking groups, educational or recreational classes, etc. – but DON'T join

Extroverts rejoice! Real estate requires you to be a social being.

People are subconsciously drawn to others they believe are "like them." By being a member of a group to which they belong, you already have an advantage over a nonmember. Moreover, scheduled meetings provide multiple opportunities to get to know each other better, unlike meeting someone at a random event or through an acquaintance.

Some opportunities to explore include:

Book clubs

Bowling leagues

Art classes

Professional networking groups

Adult education classes

Parent-teacher organizations

Charity organizations

Pilates classes

Choose a couple that fit with your interests and schedule. Just **DON'T** join.

Before You Are Licensed

If you join now, you will be meeting everyone as a computer consultant, a homemaker, an accountant, or whatever it is that you currently do. The group will quickly become more people who know that you are new to real estate and will therefore think it's risky to give you their business. There is no value in that.

However, by doing your research early, you will know exactly where to join the minute you are licensed. And guess what? You will introduce yourself to everyone as the real estate agent you are.

There will be no past history to overcome, and you can start networking immediately.

Personal Spheres to Organize Contacts into:

_____

_____

_____

_____

_____

_____

_____

_____

_____

_____

_____

_____

_____

Local Groups to Join:

_____

_____

_____

_____

_____

_____

_____

_____

_____

_____

_____

_____

_____

_____

Decide on the Fundamentals of Your Future Business

As a licensed real estate agent, more likely than not, you will be working as an independent contractor. In other words, you are in business for yourself.

So, future entrepreneur, what is your business going to look like?

10.)   Research real estate brokerages

Your biggest initial decision in real estate will be choosing a brokerage with which to hang your license.

Unlike most industries, as an independent contractor you will actually interview the brokerages – the brokerages don't solely interview you.

Call local real estate firms and request an appointment with the broker to discuss hanging your future license with the firm.

Most managing brokers will agree to meeting with you prior to being licensed. If he or she won't meet with you, do not consider hanging your license with that brokerage. Find a broker that is willing to invest time in you.

Your goal is to sort through their sales pitches (yes, they are selling you their services) and find a firm that will allow your business to thrive.

How do you determine which brokerage will help make you a success? By being honest with yourself . . . Think about what types of work environments have worked best for you in the past, and try to find a similar model.

Just like agents, brokerages come in all shapes and sizes.

Decide on the Fundamentals of Your Future Business

What to consider when to choosing a brokerage:

Physical Office:

Is it in close proximity to your home?

Is it in close proximity to where you wish to sell?

Is there a receptionist to greet your clients?

Is there adequate parking for your clients?

Are there conference rooms?

Are computers available?

Are you able to have a designated desk?

Can you rent a private office?

Is there support staff to assist the agents?

Is it clean and inviting?

The agents:

How many agents are there?

Is there an expectation of cooperation?

Are agents friendly?

Do agents typically stay for a few years?

Is there one top agent that gets special treatment?

Do agents seem highly competitive?

Are there awards and sales contests visible?

Before You Are Licensed

Community involvement:

Are the agents encouraged to be visible and charitable in the community?

Does the brokerage support charitable organizations in the community?

Commission structure:

Compared to other brokerages, how does the commission split compare?

Is there a monthly fee?

Is there a transaction fee?

Is there a technology fee?

Is your errors and omission insurance included?

Is there a sign-on (joining) fee?

Do they pay for your signage, open house flyers, home photography, business cards, headshots, etc.?

Once you begin producing, is there a number at which you can cap on commission or renegotiate your commission?

Do they provide and pay for training? Is it more marketing or contract/transaction based? Are contract classes taught by attorneys?

Is a mentor provided? If so, are you required to split commissions with the mentor? How many sales and at what percentage?

Decide on the Fundamentals of Your Future Business

Name recognition:

> If it's an older firm, is the name quickly recognized in the local area?

> Is the name respected?

Technology:

> What type of technology is provided, if any?

> Is training included?

> Do they provide a website?

> Do they provide Customer Relationship Management (CRM) software?

> Are you required to work within the technology, or is it optional?

> If you pay for the technology, could you take it with you if you ever switched brokerages?

Broker Involvement:

> Is the broker a competing broker, meaning he also sells homes himself?

> Who will be checking your contracts and files for compliance?

> If you have a question, whom should you call? What times are they available for you?

Does the broker personally work with new agents regarding goal setting and business plans?

Do you care for the broker's personality?

Do you believe the broker to be knowledgeable?

Company Philosophy:

While not all brokerages actually follow their published philosophy, it would be wise to read it. Does it align with how you wish to conduct real estate?

For new agents, I suggest focusing less on commission and more on training and broker support. If you become a strong agent and start closing deals, you can always renegotiate your commission.

Training should include legal seminars, contract classes, federal regulation courses, etc. — education of substance, if you will. Marketing classes are valuable, but can be found anywhere, from books to online. If it's a larger firm, it likely has a calendar of classes. Ask to review it and try to gauge the ratio of substance vs. marketing classes.

Moreover, as a new agent, you should look for a cooperative environment in which to learn. By being able to ask questions of others and watch how they solve problems in different scenarios, you will learn exponentially.

With regard to name recognition, study after study shows the brokerage name is rarely the reason a client will choose to work with you. Do not allow the firm's name to weigh heavily in your decision unless the firm has a bad reputation.

11.)   Sit with an accountant

The amount of time you can save by talking with your accountant before you begin practicing real estate is immeasurable.

A quick (and hopefully free) consultation is all you need.

Questions to ask:

> Do you have clients in real estate?
>
> Do you suggest a certain corporate structure (LLC, PA, Sole Proprietorship)?
>
> If recommended, how will I go about registering as that type of structure?
>
> Should I keep a separate business bank account?
>
> How do you suggest I write off my car (mileage or depreciation/maintenance)?
>
> What other deductions will I likely be able to take as a real estate agent?
>
> Is there any accounting software you recommend?

The answers will dictate what to do next.

Perhaps you will need to compare different banks' small business account fees and required minimum balances. You might need to purchase and learn new software.

Before You Are Licensed

Have a plan about how to handle your finances from the start. Stopping your business activities each April to sort through a shoe box of receipts, failing to get every deduction possible, and paying late filing fees *is not* a business plan. It's an expensive waste of time.

Decide on the Fundamentals of Your Future Business

Local Real Estate Brokerages to Interview with:

_____
_____
_____
_____
_____
_____
_____
_____
_____
_____
_____
_____
_____
_____

Accountant Suggestions to Implement:

_____
_____
_____
_____
_____
_____
_____
_____
_____
_____
_____
_____
_____
_____
_____

Plan Your Marketing Strategy

Once you are licensed, the quicker you can get yourself in front of the public, the better. Too many new agents either completely fail to market themselves in their first year or waste money marketing without a clear message or brand. If you want success, you will need to market quickly, consistently, *and* strategically.

12.) Select and research a niche

A new agent who chooses to focus on a niche is likely to find early success. Why? Because by hyper-focusing on an additional small niche at the same time as you acquire general market knowledge, you will quickly be able to distinguish yourself from other agents as an expert (in that one niche at least). The quicker you can stand out from the crowd – the better.

A few of the hundreds of niches to choose from include:

Prairie-style homes

New construction

Ski chalets

Student housing alternatives

Condos

Seniors

Foreign investors

Fly-in communities

First-time homebuyers

Another benefit of working a niche is that it allows for targeted marketing. Your marketing will be created for, and solely distributed to, those in your niche. This will result in both a reduced cost and a higher conversion rate. You won't be throwing generic ads into the universe. You will be sending people already interested in your message a reason to do business with you. What could be better?

Once you have chosen a niche, begin to study it both academically and physically within your community.

Each time you learn an interesting aspect about your niche, write approximately 1,000 words about it. Rinse and repeat numerous times. Not only will you be learning, you will also be creating a library of posts for your future real estate blog.

While out and about in the community, remember to photograph anything that relates to your niche. File away your photos for later use in advertisements, social media, and blogs.

Moreover, search stock photos relating to your niche to be saved alongside your personal photos. Be careful to only use photos with a "Creative Commons" license, without which you would need the photographer's written permission to use the photo.

For example, should you decide your niche will be servicing veterans:

Learn and write about what services and benefits your town offers veterans.

Is there a base in the area? Can you arrange to take a tour?

Study in depth and then later summarize for a future post how Veterans Administration loans work.

Take a local veteran to lunch. Ask him or her what housing needs, concerns, or situations are common for veterans. The answers will prompt subjects for your writing.

Attend and photograph the next Memorial Day parade in your town.

Photograph the flag outside your local school or municipal buildings.

Collect some Creative Commons license photos of the Vietnam War Memorial, the Tomb of the Unknowns, etc.

Before you know it, you will have learned a wealth of information to share with future clients, *and* have a library of original blogs and social media posts to leisurely pick from once you are licensed (and too busy to create them from scratch).

13.) Decide on your personal branding

How do you want the public to perceive you in your real estate role? If you had to pick one adjective, what would it be?

Professional

Competent

Trustworthy

Ethical

Approachable

Kind

Other?

Once you have selected your adjective, all your branding should fall into place.

Every marketing piece you will ever write, every blog you will ever post, every email you will ever send, and every business card you will ever print will reflect that adjective.

Furthermore, because you were savvy enough to learn a niche, you will pair your adjective *with* your niche for highly memorable marketing.

Remember, the key to successful marketing is consistency; stay true to your brand and niche.

If your adjective was "Approachable," and your niche was "Ski chalets," I would expect:

Before You Are Licensed

A headshot with you dressed in business casual or ski gear.

Blogs and social media posts written in a conversational style and sprinkled with occasional ski jargon. Beyond real estate articles, there would be the occasional discussion regarding snow conditions and ski equipment reviews.

Your email signoff would likely be "Talk soon," and your voice mail would have any easygoing air to it.

Your tagline would be reflective as well: "Your mountaintop specialist."

I see new agent marketing unravel the most because of the headshot. Unless, of course, the adjective was:

Exotic dancer (Yes, I said it!)

Goofball

Thug

Partier

Assuming the brokerage you plan to join does not include headshots in their sign-on package, hire a professional photographer to get them done. Make certain you are provided with both high resolution (for print marketing) and low resolution (for web) images.

Niches to Consider:

_____

_____

_____

_____

_____

_____

_____

_____

_____

_____

_____

_____

_____

_____

_____

Personal Branding Adjectives to Contemplate:

_____

_____

_____

_____

_____

_____

_____

_____

_____

_____

_____

_____

_____

_____

Conclusion, or Actually, Beginning...

I do hope you use your pre-license time to the fullest. As you'll soon learn as an agent, time is precious. Take control of your future. And once you obtain your license – hit the ground running!

About the Author

Katherine Scarim, her amazing husband of over 20 years, and their five children live in sunny Jupiter, Florida.

Katherine grew up dreaming of being a real estate agent (just checking if you were still reading – that would have been something, huh? She probably wanted to be veterinarian or a candy maker . . .)

Katherine's brokerage, Island Bridge Realty, was conceived as her vision of how real estate should be. She hopes she will leave the Real Estate Industry a little better than she found it.

Island Bridge Realty's Philosophy

Always exceed industry standards and be the *Source* of real estate knowledge.

Never sanction mediocrity or incompetence.

Always be open to change and new ideas.

Work cooperatively to make certain our clients' goals are achieved.

Firmly believe the Whole is greater than the sum of its parts.

Recognize the importance of a full-time, non-competing broker whose focus is heavily on agent support and education.

Work within our communities to re-energize the local economy and maintain local charm.

Stay true to our philosophy, and remain a boutique, locally owned firm.

Thank you for reading this book!

I do hope you found it valuable.

It is my passion to help aspiring real estate agents across the country. If you are looking for additional support to help your future career, please visit AGENTSTRONG.COM to learn more about my online coaching/training programs. The AGENT LAUNCH 12 Week Program was especially designed for new agents to supplement their brokerage training.

Also check out <u>Dear Real Estate Agent: There are Answers</u>, a book I co-authored with a real estate attorney, a home inspector, an insurance agent, a mortgage broker and a business attorney to help agents understand their role as the generalist in a sea of specialists.

Reach out to me with any questions, suggestions, and success stories! Don't be shy. I would truly love to hear from you. Email me at <u>Katherine@AgentStrong.com</u> or connect with me on LinkedIn <u>https://www.linkedin.com/in/katherinescarim</u>

As a personal favor, would you be so kind as to leave a review on Amazon?

Thank you.

25496409R00031

Made in the USA
San Bernardino, CA
11 February 2019